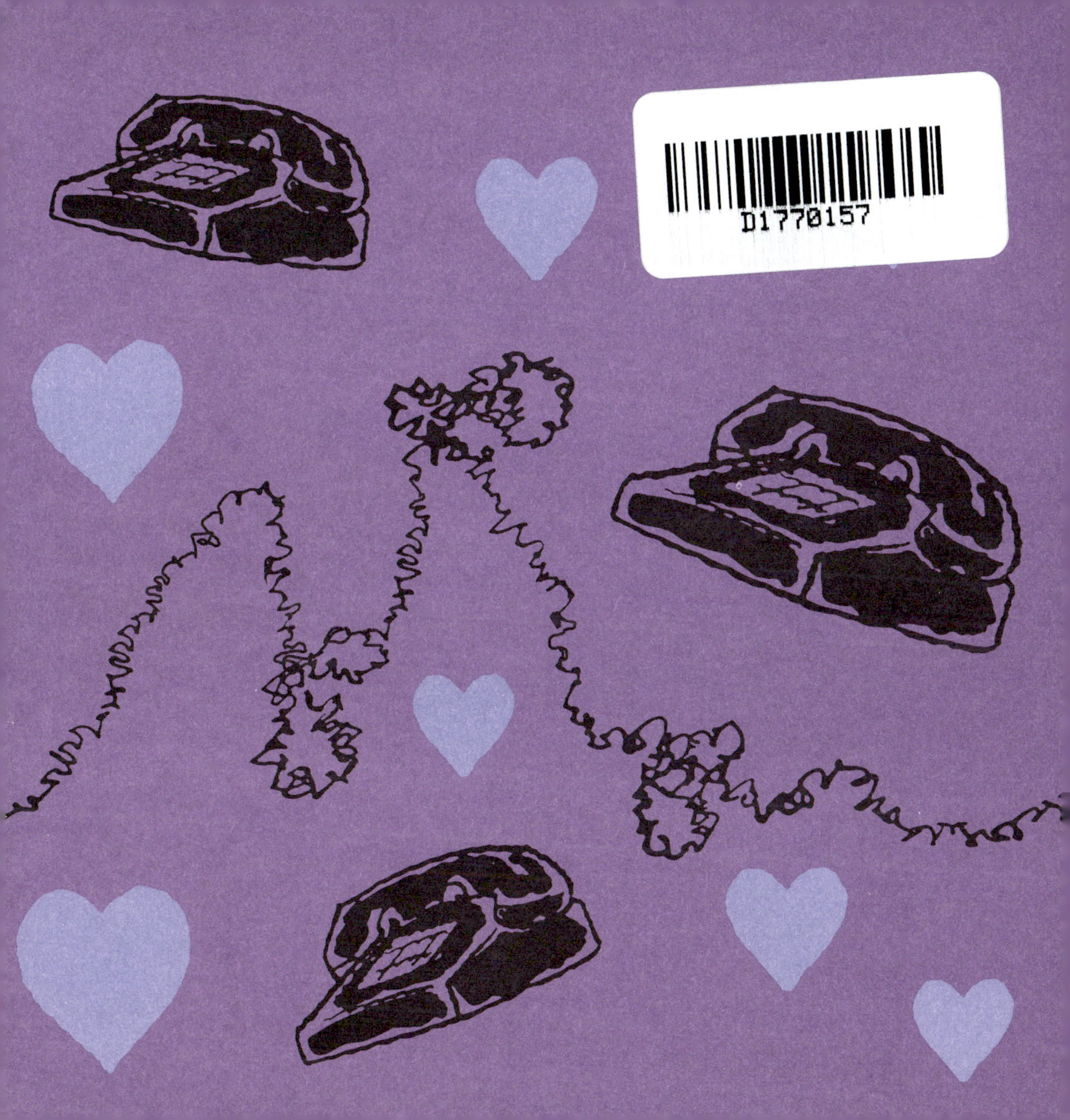

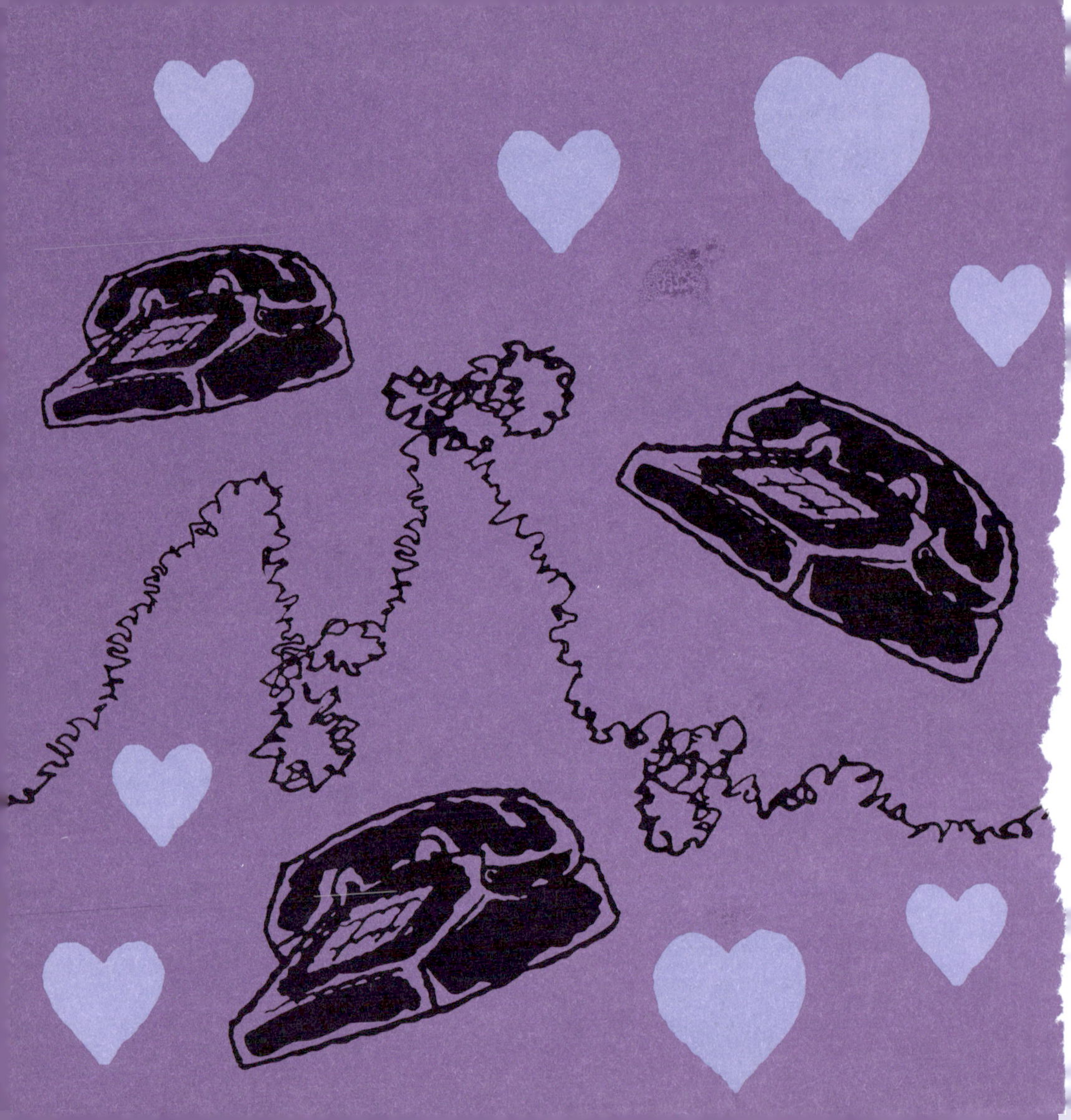

Our Lines Must Be Crossed!

by
SCHULZ

HarperHorizon
An Imprint of HarperCollins*Publishers*

If Love Is A Language, It's Foreign To Me!

HI, CHUCK.. I JUST GOT HOME FROM CAMP, AND THOUGHT I'D RUN OVER TO SEE IF YOU MISSED ME...
IF I WHAT?
MISSED ME! YOU KNOW, FELT ABANDONED..PINED AWAY THE HOURS..LIFE LOST ITS MEANING.. THAT SORT OF THING...
WELL..

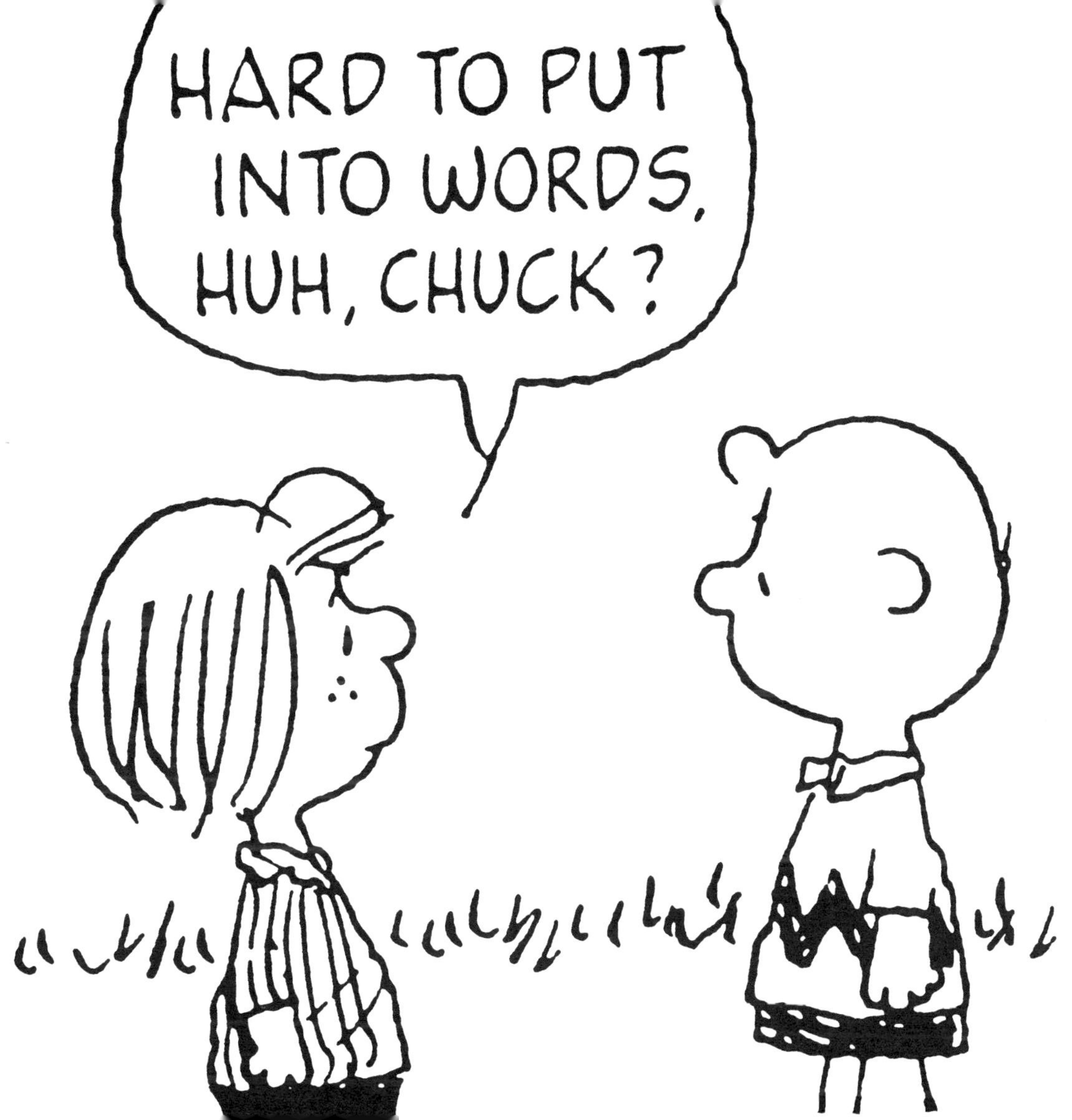
HARD TO PUT INTO WORDS, HUH, CHUCK?

HI, CHARLES! I JUST GOT BACK..I CALLED YOU SEVERAL TIMES... DID YOU MISS ME?
I JUST POURED MYSELF SOME COLD CEREAL..I DON'T WANT IT TO GET SOGGY...
AAUGH!

If Love Is A Language, It's Foreign To Me!

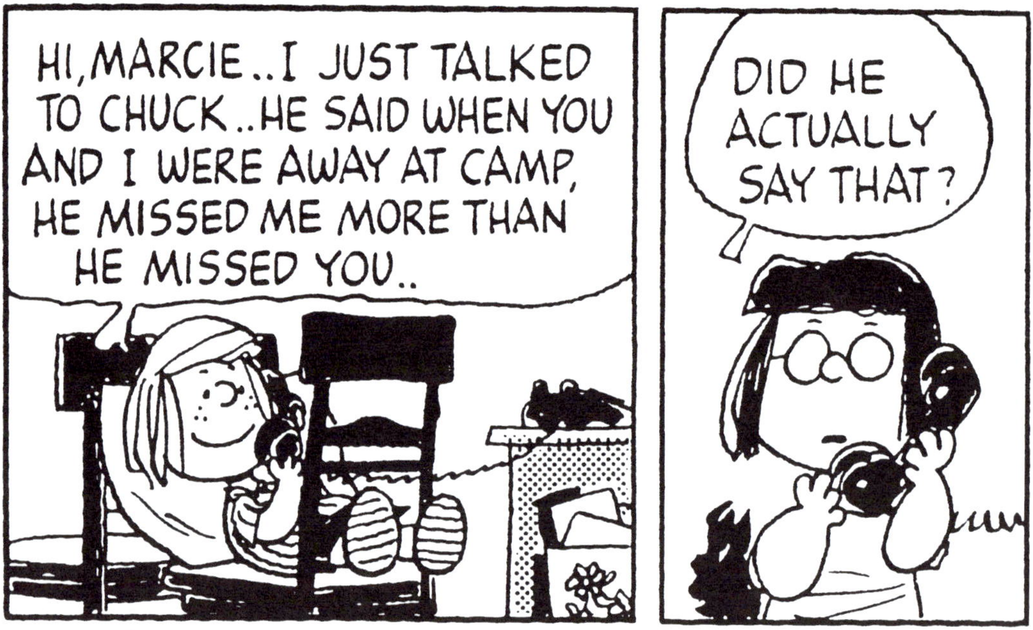
HI, MARCIE .. I JUST TALKED TO CHUCK .. HE SAID WHEN YOU AND I WERE AWAY AT CAMP, HE MISSED ME MORE THAN HE MISSED YOU ..
DID HE ACTUALLY SAY THAT?

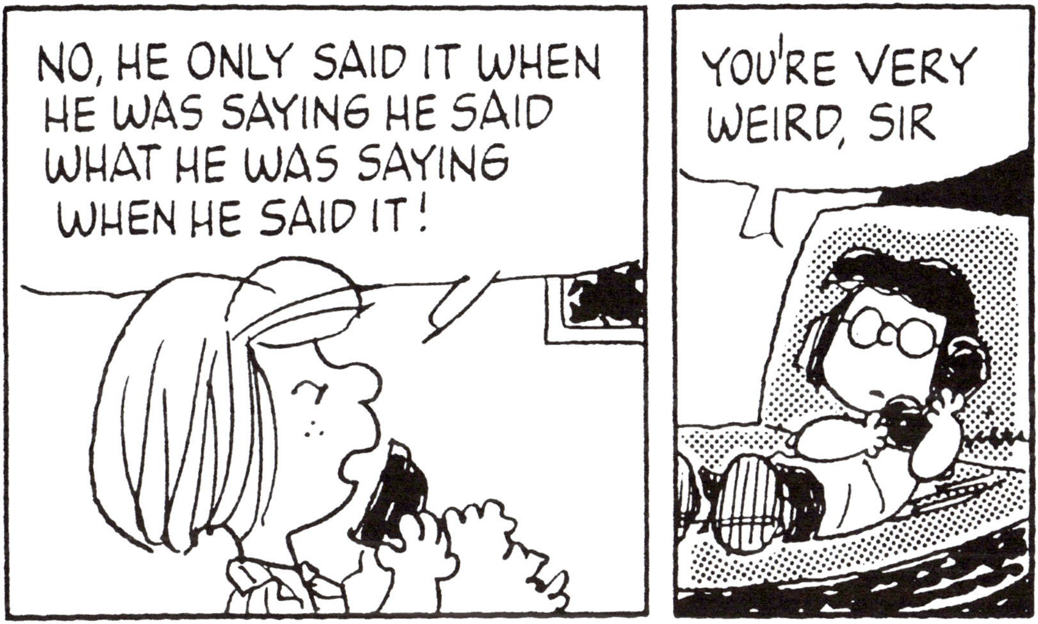
NO, HE ONLY SAID IT WHEN HE WAS SAYING HE SAID WHAT HE WAS SAYING WHEN HE SAID IT!
YOU'RE VERY WEIRD, SIR

YOU KNOW, WHEN WE WERE AWAY AT CAMP, I DON'T THINK CHUCK MISSED EITHER ONE OF US
I WONDER WHAT WE COULD SAY TO LET HIM KNOW HOW THAT MADE US FEEL...TO LET HIM KNOW WE'RE SENSITIVE

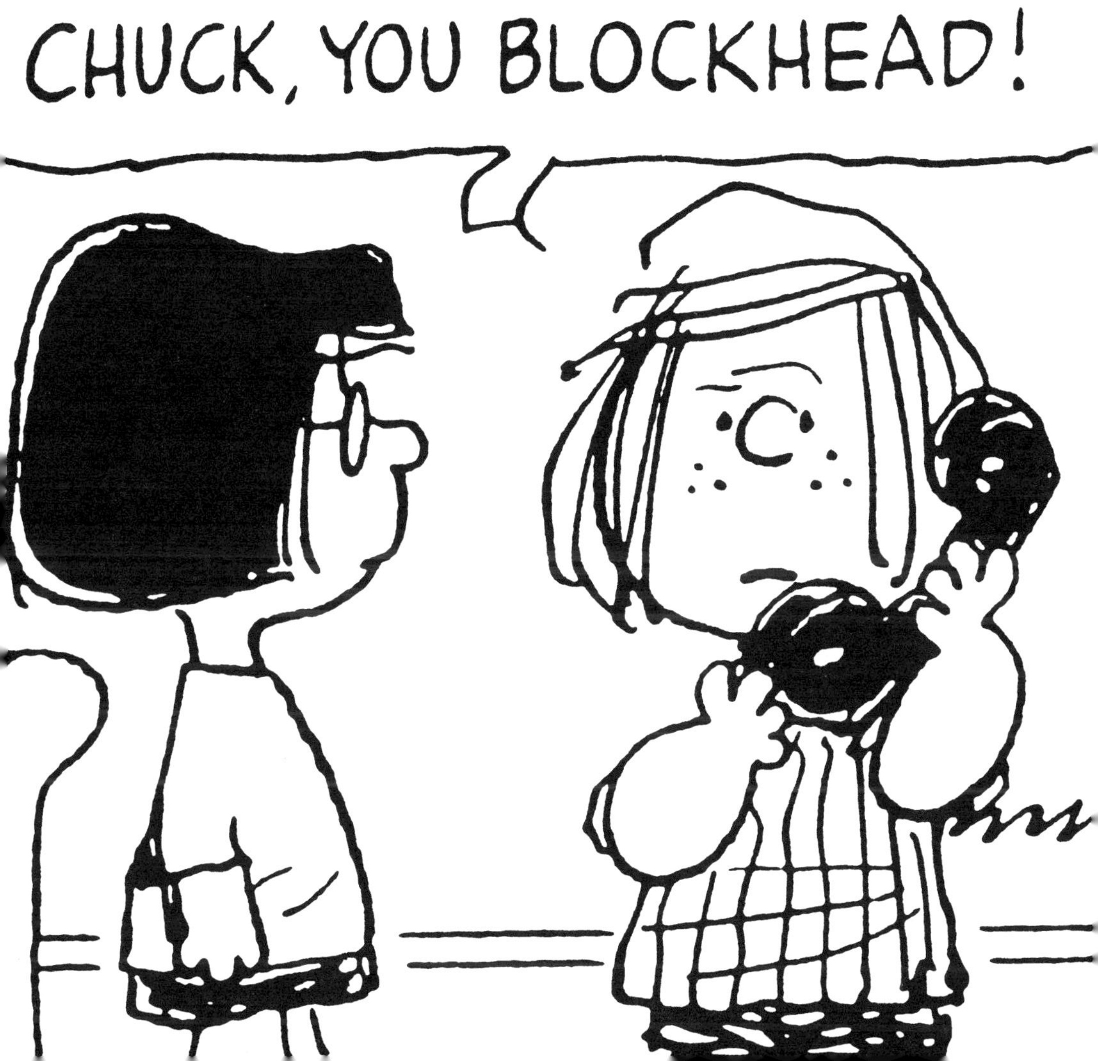
CHUCK, YOU BLOCKHEAD!

Mixed Messages

DID YOU FALL IN LOVE THE FIRST TIME YOU SAW ME ?
NO, YOU DIDN'T IMPRESS ME THAT MUCH
HOW ABOUT NOW? HOW DO YOU FEEL NOW WHEN YOU LOOK AT ME?
WELL, WHEN I TWIST AROUND LIKE THIS, IT SORT OF HURTS MY NECK..

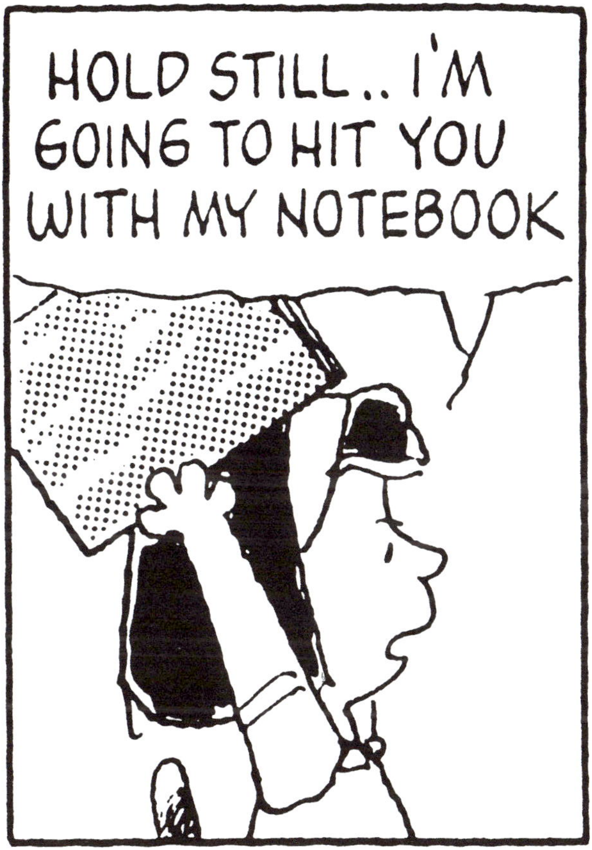
HOLD STILL.. I'M GOING TO HIT YOU WITH MY NOTEBOOK

LYDIA, COULD I BORROW A PAPER CLIP?
AREN'T YOU KIND OF OLD FOR ME?
I DIDN'T ASK YOU TO MARRY ME! I JUST WANT A PAPER CLIP!

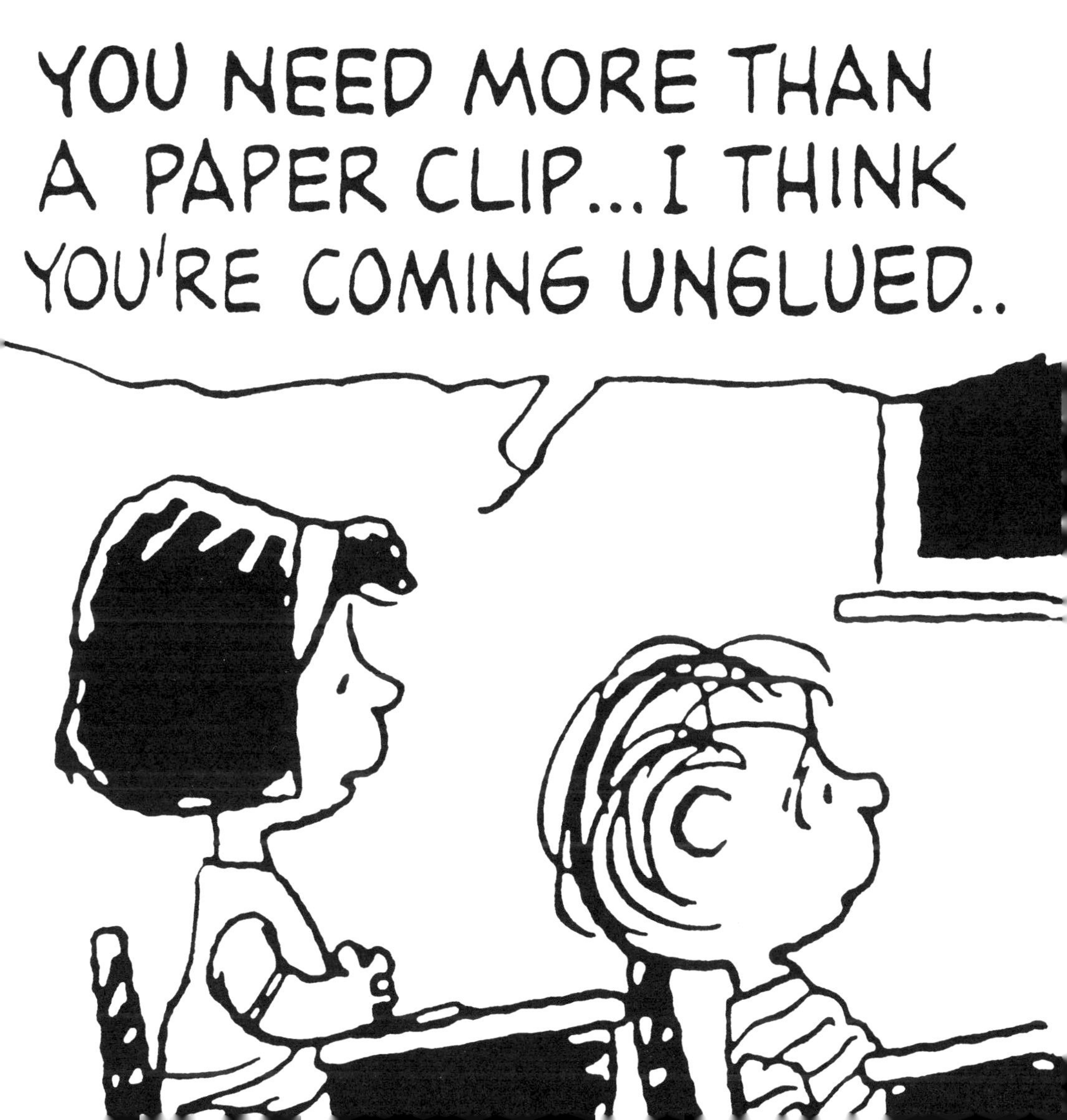
YOU NEED MORE THAN A PAPER CLIP... I THINK YOU'RE COMING UNGLUED..

I THINK A MUSIC BOX IS THE MOST ROMANTIC GIFT THAT A BOY CAN GIVE TO A GIRL..
HOW ABOUT HALF OF A PEANUT BUTTER SANDWICH?

WHAT SONG DOES IT PLAY ?

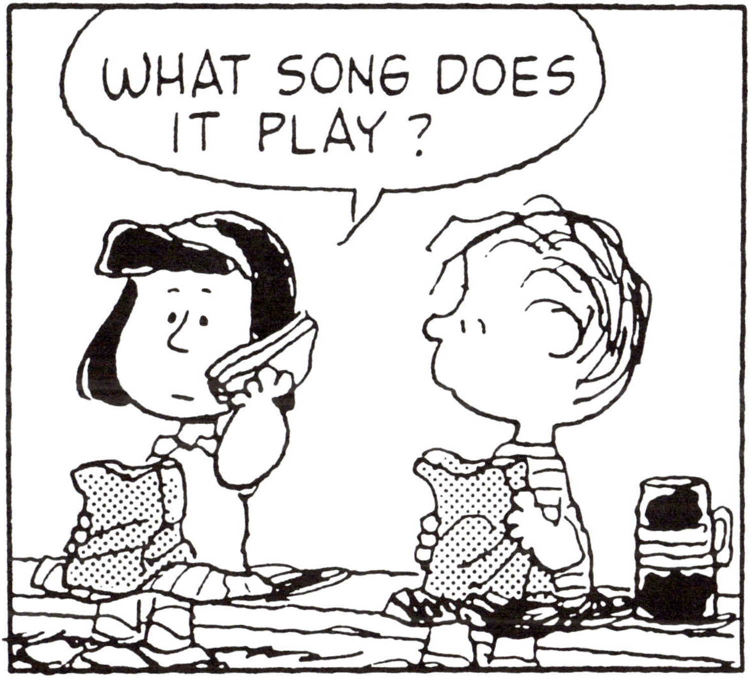

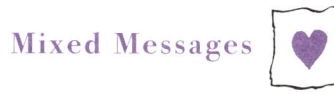

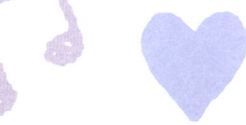

A MUSIC BOX! LINUS, YOU BOUGHT ME A MUSIC BOX!
WELL, YOU SAID A MUSIC BOX IS THE MOST ROMANTIC GIFT THAT A BOY CAN GIVE TO A GIRL..
IT IS! IT'S VERY SPECIAL..

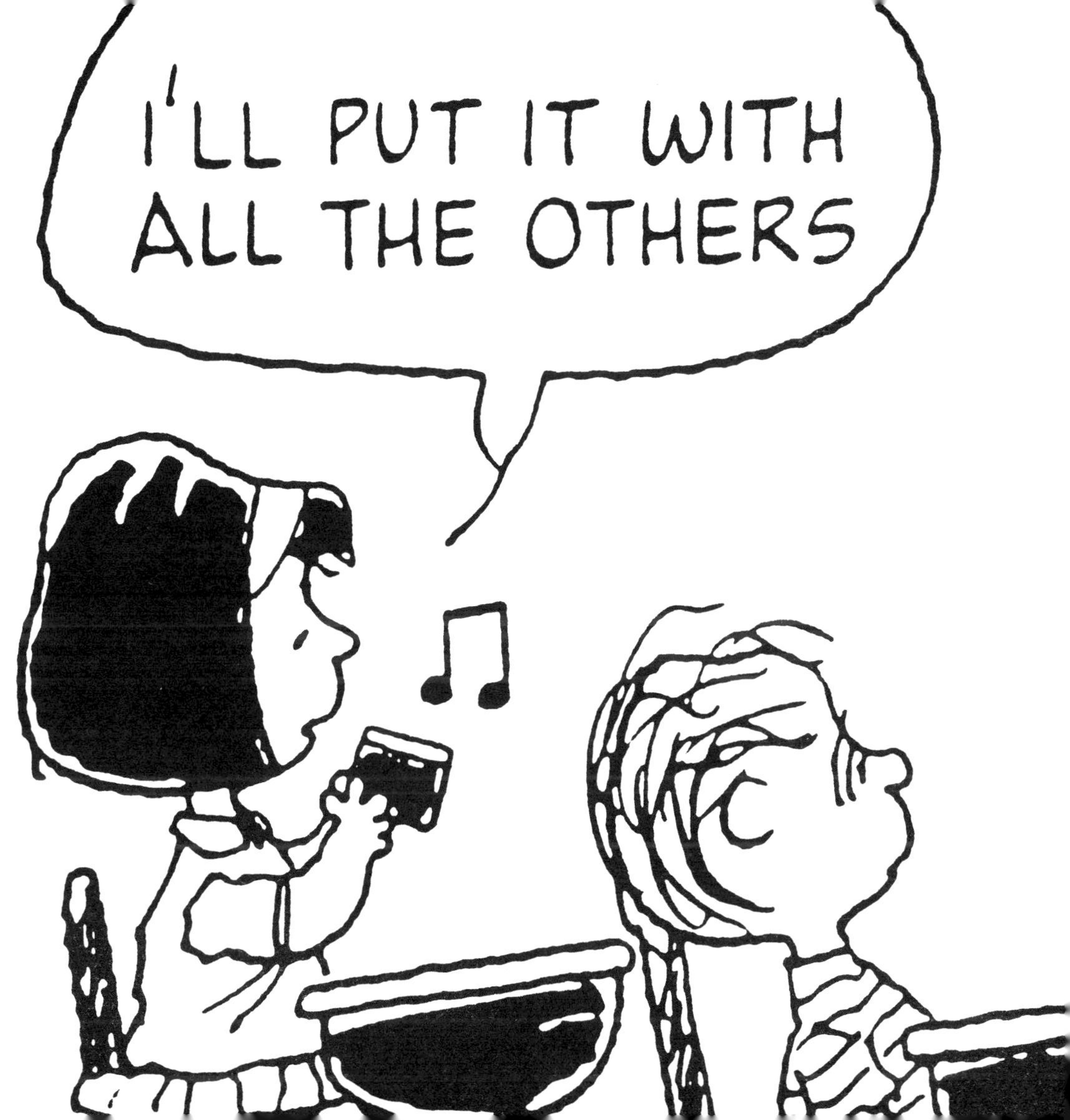
I'LL PUT IT WITH ALL THE OTHERS

Listening In

MUSICIANS PLAY A LOT OF LOVE SONGS, BUT THEY DON'T REALLY HEAR THEM, DO THEY?

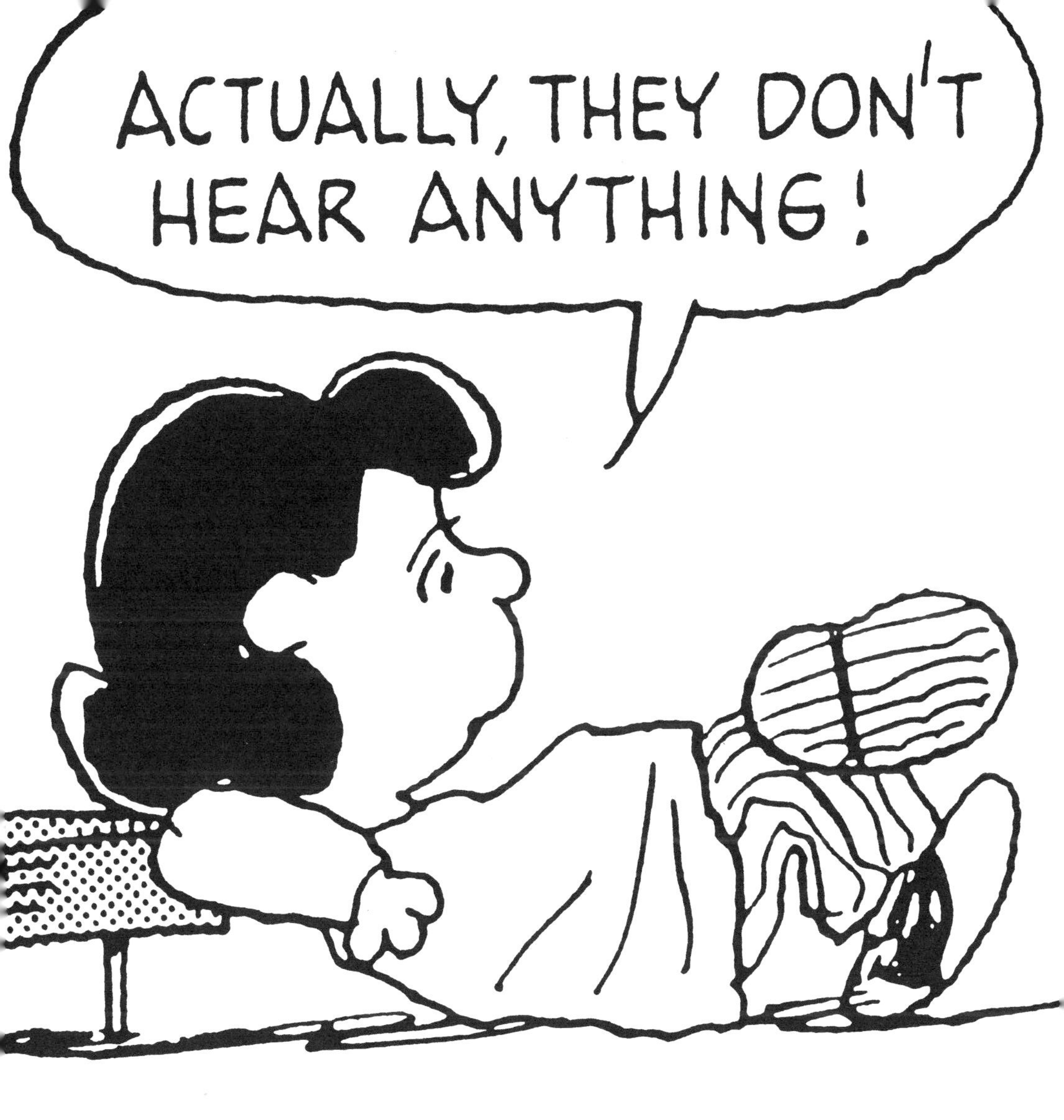
ACTUALLY, THEY DON'T HEAR ANYTHING!

Listening In

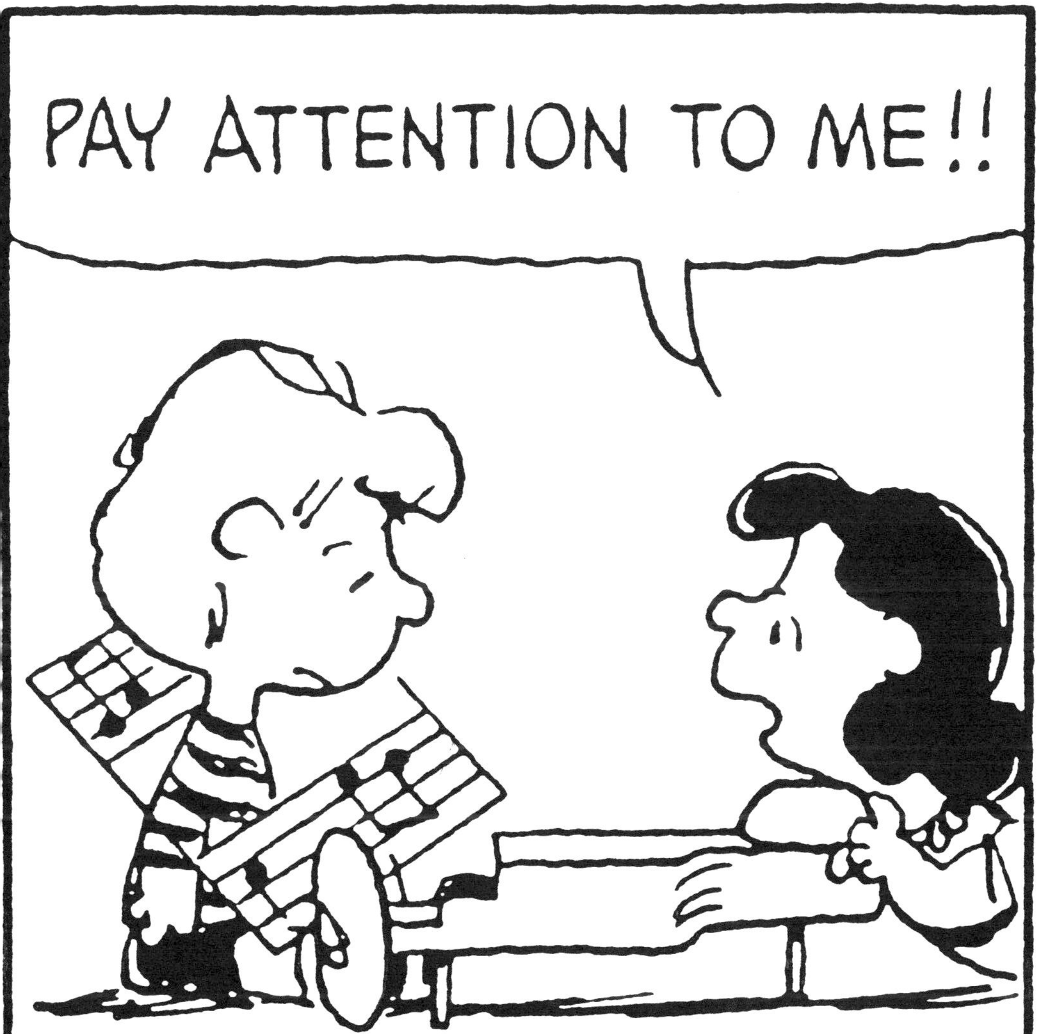
PAY ATTENTION TO ME!!

HERE'S THE WAY I SEE IT...IF YOU TRULY THINK I'M BEAUTIFUL, THEN YOU SHOULD TELL ME...
IF YOU DON'T THINK I'M BEAUTIFUL, I'D RATHER NOT KNOW...JUST DON'T SAY ANYTHING...

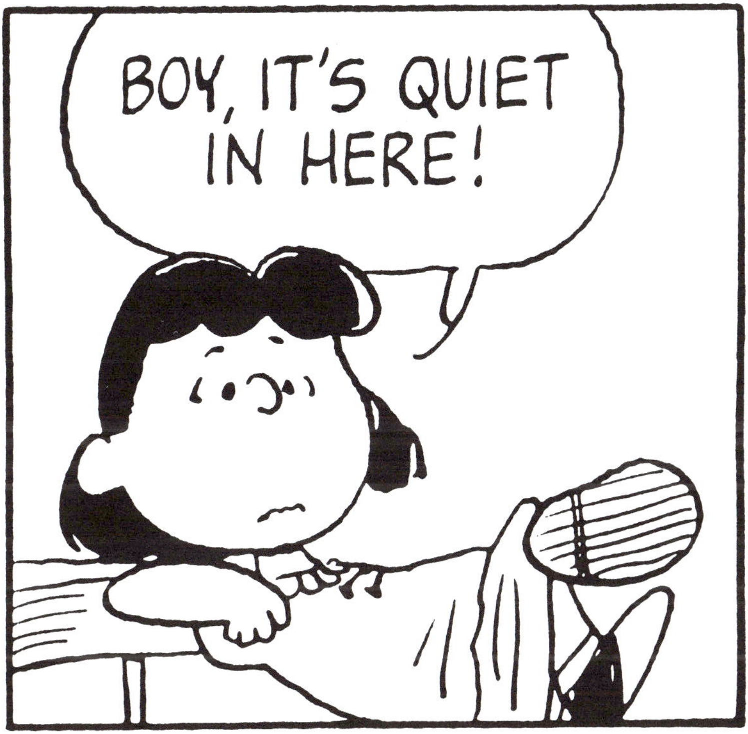
BOY, IT'S QUIET IN HERE!

HEY, PITCHER..TELL YOUR CATCHER I THINK HE'S KIND OF CUTE..
TELL YOUR RIGHT FIELDER I THINK SHE'S INSANE..
SHE SAYS SHE THINKS YOU'RE KIND OF CUTE, AND HE SAYS HE THINKS YOU'RE INSANE..

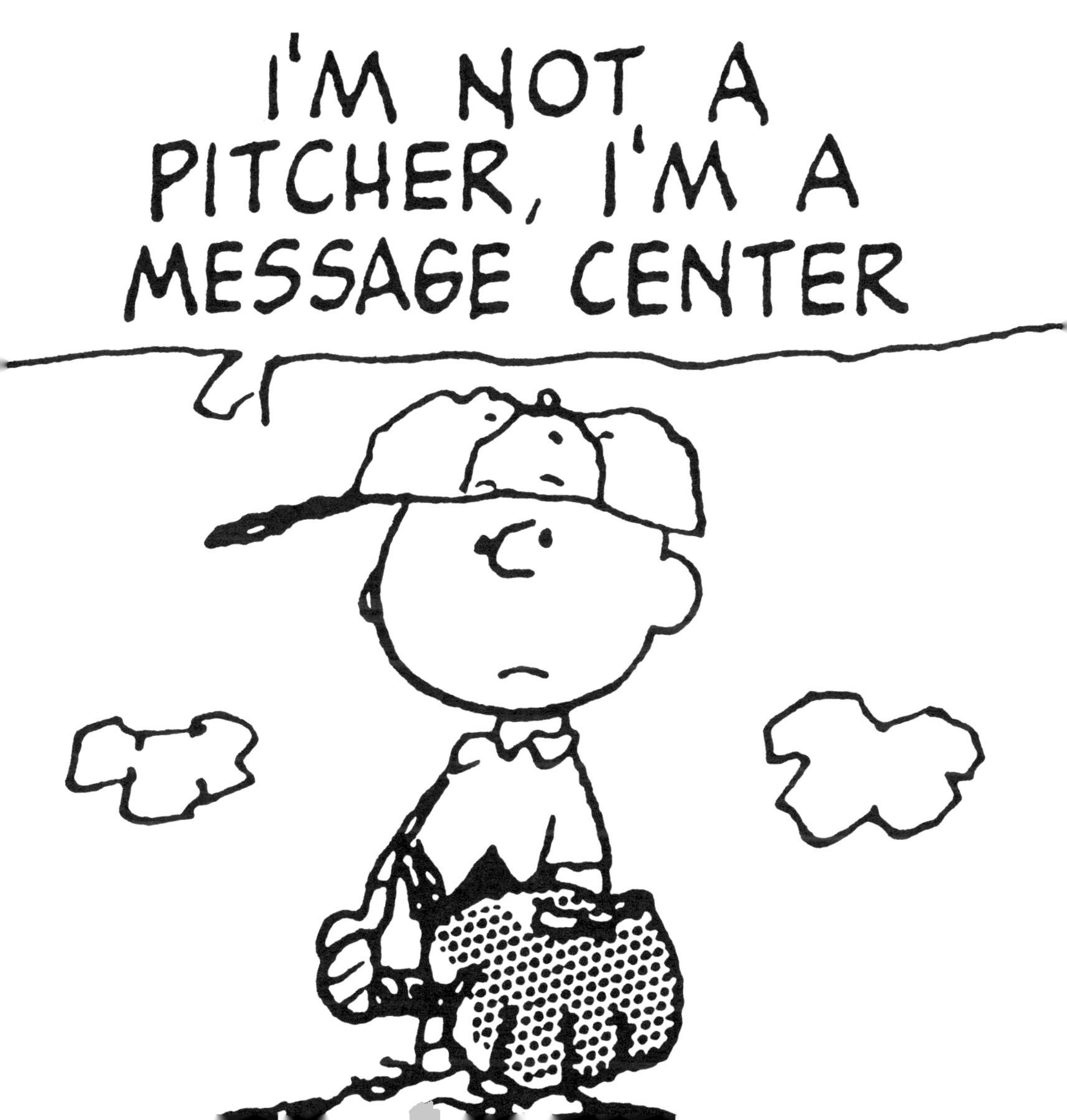
I'M NOT A PITCHER, I'M A MESSAGE CENTER

❤ HarperHorizon
An Imprint of HarperCollins*Publishers*

Produced by Jennifer Barry Design, Sausalito, CA
First published in 1998 by HarperCollins*Publishers* Inc.
http://www.harpercollins.com
Copyright © 1998 United Feature Syndicate, Inc. All rights reserved.
HarperCollins ® and ❤ ® are trademarks of HarperCollins*Publishers* Inc.
Our Lines Must Be Crossed! was published by HarperHorizon, an imprint of
HarperCollins*Publishers* Inc., 10 East 53rd Street, New York, NY 10022.
Horizon is a registered trademark used under license from Forbes Inc.
PEANUTS is a registered trademark of United Feature Syndicate, Inc.
PEANUTS © United Feature Syndicate, Inc.
Based on the PEANUTS ® comic strip by Charles M. Schulz
http://www.unitedmedia.com

ISBN 0-06-757451-3

Printed in Hong Kong

1 3 5 7 9 10 8 6 4 2

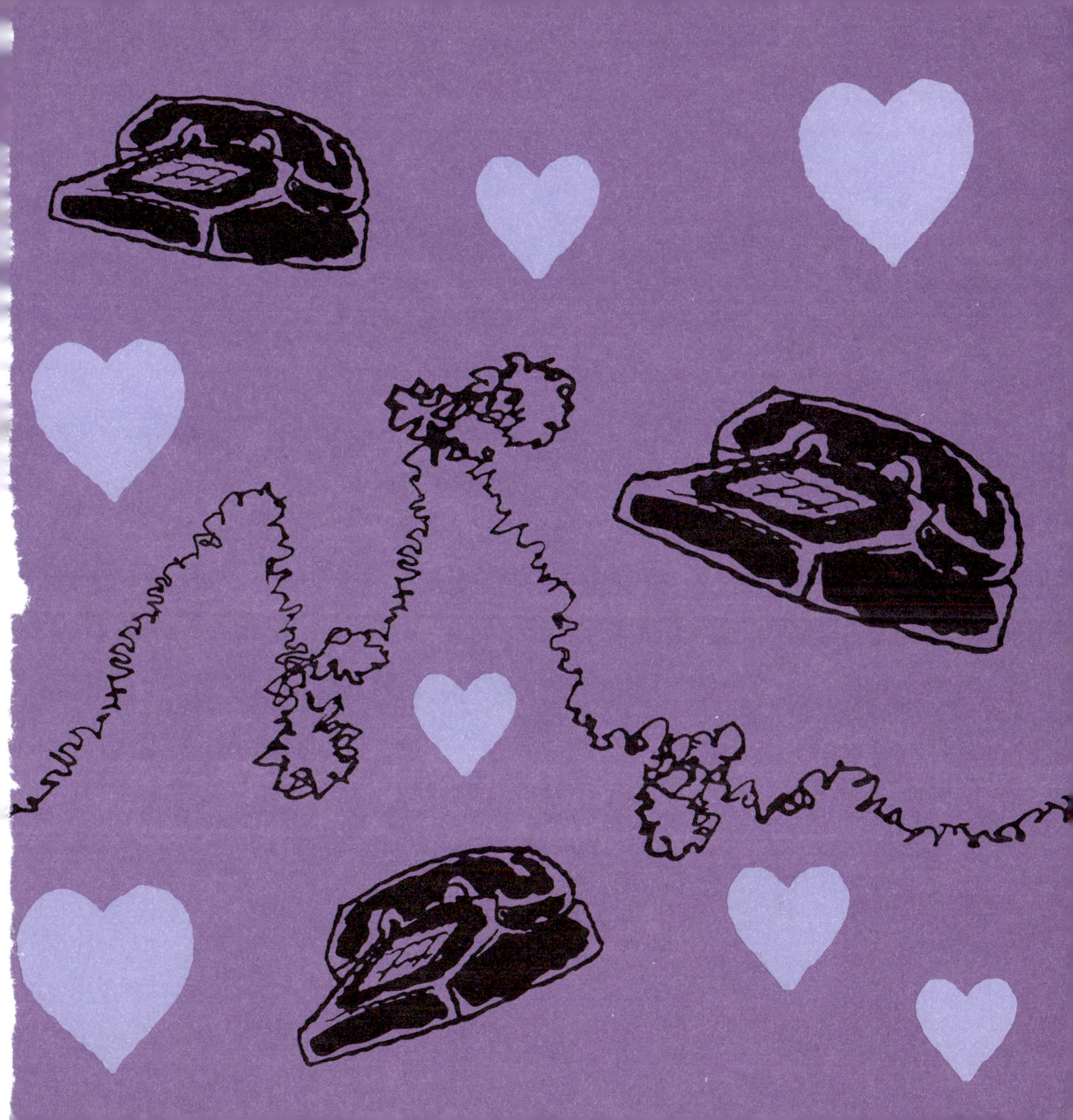

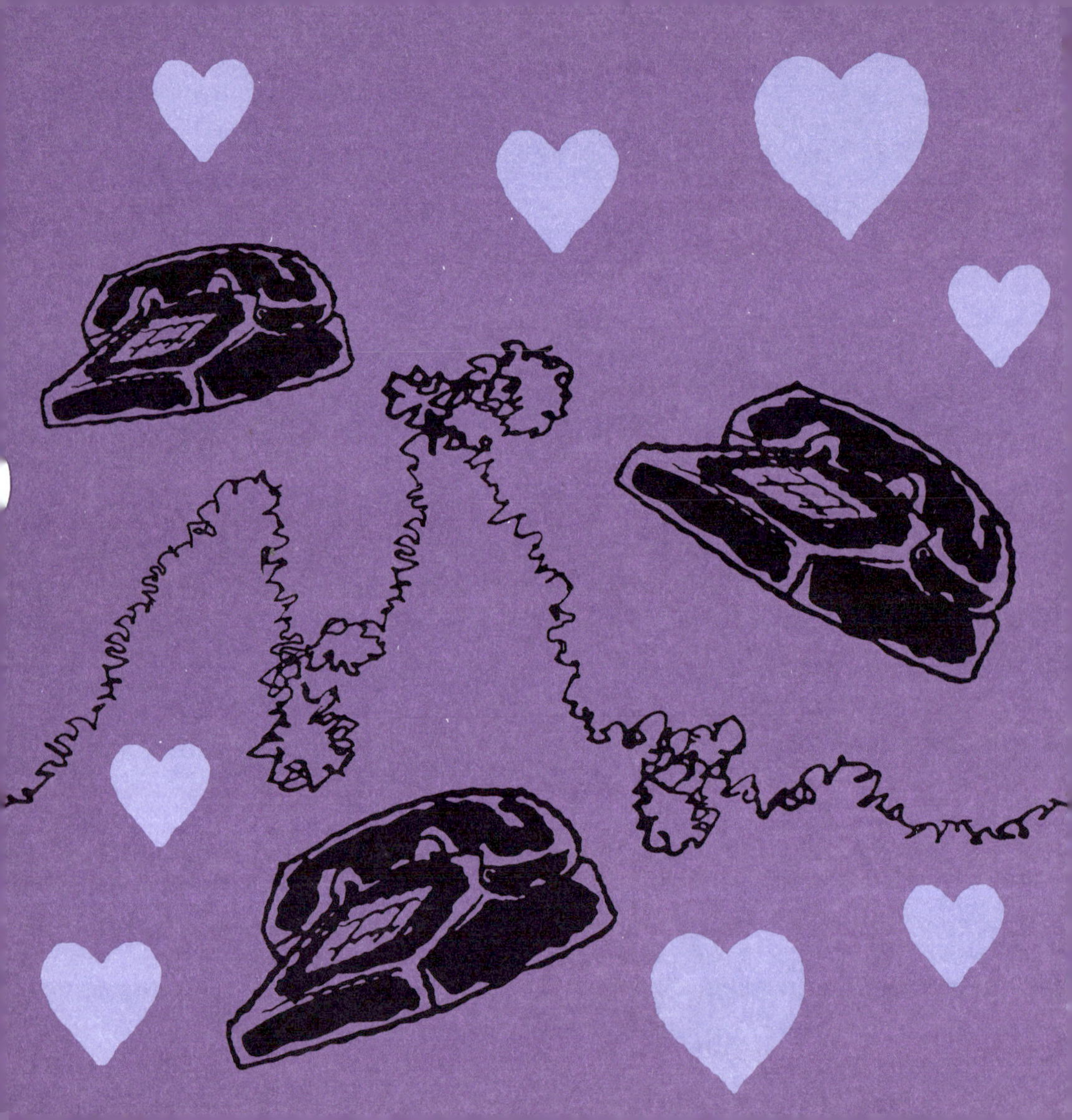